Zip it!

How do you keep
a jacket shut?

How do you stop things from tipping out of a backpack?

A zip (or zipper) will do the job and do it well!

A zip keeps things shut
and keeps things in.

There are zips on lots of
things such as purses,
bags, boots and tents.

A zip can be added to all sorts of fabrics.

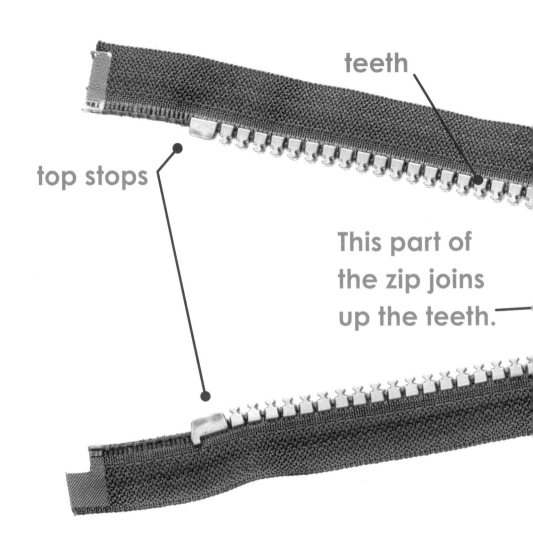

teeth

top stops

This part of
the zip joins
up the teeth.

A zip has tracks that
look a bit like teeth.

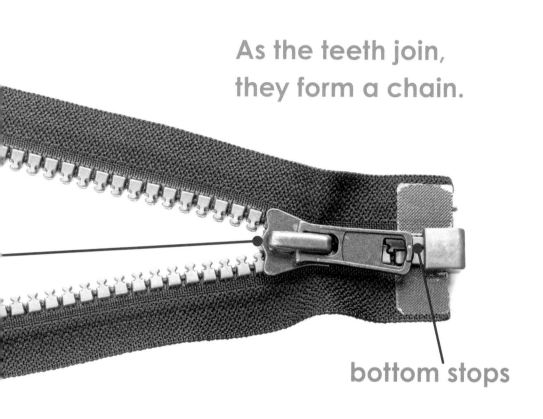

As the teeth join, they form a chain.

bottom stops

If the teeth are interlocked, then the zip is shut. A shut zip is hard to split.

We have had zips for longer than one hundred years!

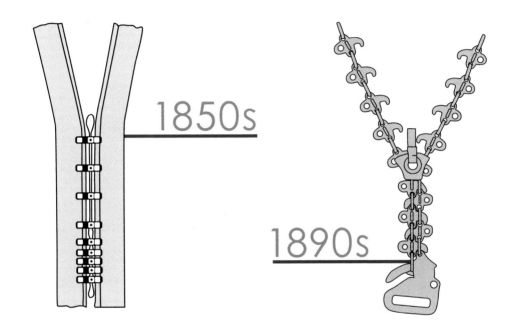

1850s

1890s

In 1891, the zip was invented but it was not much like a zip now.

In 1913, the sort of zip we see now was invented.

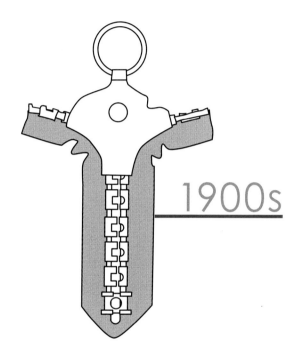

1900s

Back in the 1920s, zips went on boots. In the 1930s, they went on children's outfits.

Buttons are hard for little children to do up. Zips are best!

Fun zip fact!

"Zip" is said to have come from the "zip" that you hear as you zip up.

Will you zip up or
button up next?

No zip? No problem! You
still have buttons and belts.

Zip it!

Dad tells us to "zip it" if we are chatting in bed!

Words to blend

look	boots	how
zipper	interlocked	longer
keeps	teeth	purses
sorts	join	chain
hard	hear	fact
problem	invented	next
tracks	stops	still

Before reading

Synopsis: We probably all have clothes or other items that have zips to open and close. But have there always been zips?

Review graphemes/phonemes: oo oo ow er ee ur or oi ai ar ear

Story discussion: Look at the cover and read the title together. Ask: *What do you think this book is going to be about? What sort of information do you think it might give us about zips?* Briefly flick through and elicit that the book includes information on how zips work, what they are used for and where we find them.

Link to prior learning: Display a word with adjacent consonants from the story, e.g. *children*. Ask children to put a dot under each single-letter grapheme (*i, l, d, r, e, n*) and a line under the digraph (*ch*). Model, if necessary, how to sound out and blend the adjacent consonants together to read the word. Repeat with another word from the story, e.g. *tracks*, and encourage children to sound out and blend the word independently.

Vocabulary check: interlocked – fitting tightly together

Decoding practice: Display the word *invented*. Show children how to split it into three syllables: *in/vent/ed*. Together, sound out and blend each syllable in turn, to read the word.

Tricky word practice: Display the word *there*. Read the word, and ask children to show you the tricky bit (*ere*, which makes the sound /air/). Practise reading and spelling this word.

After reading

Apply learning: Ask: *What new information have you found out about zips from this book?* Encourage children to find or recall at least one fact they didn't know before reading.

Comprehension

- How many different things that use zips can you remember from the book?

- Where does the word *zip* come from?

- Do you prefer clothes with zips or buttons? Why?

Fluency

- Pick a page that most of the group read quite easily. Ask them to reread it with pace and expression. Model how to do this if necessary.

- Encourage children to choose the page from the book that they found most interesting, and read it with appropriate pace and intonation.

- Practise reading the words on page 17.

Tricky words review

do	you	out
of	there	are
be	all	they
we	have	like
said	no	was